CONTENTS

4–5 WHAT IS LIFE?

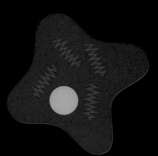

6–7 CLASSIFYING LIFE

8–9 MOVEMENT

10–11 GROWTH

12–13 REPRODUCTION

14–15 BODY SHAPES

16–17 CELLS

18–19 LIVING TOGETHER

20–21 LIVING IN WATER

22–23 LIVING ON LAND

24–25 FOOD CHAINS AND WEBS

26–27 CIRCLE OF LIFE

28–29 EVOLUTION AND ADAPTATION

30–31 GLOSSARY & WEBSITES

32 INDEX

WELCOME TO THE WORLD OF INFOGRAPHICS

Using icons, graphics and pictograms, infographics visualise information in a whole new way!

SEE HOW DEEP A TREE'S ROOTS CAN GROW.

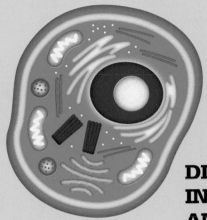

DISCOVER WHAT'S INSIDE TINY ANIMAL CELLS.

READ ABOUT HOW SOME ANIMALS SWING THROUGH THE TREES.

FIND OUT ABOUT THE LARGEST LIVING THING ON THE PLANET.

WHAT IS LIFE?

Living things come in a wide range of shapes, types and sizes. While the tiniest are too small for the human eye to see, the biggest cover huge areas.

DEFINITION
There is no set definition for life, but living things show some if not all of these characteristics.

REGULATE THEIR BODIES

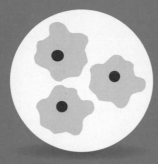

ARE COMPOSED OF ONE OR MORE CELLS

PRODUCE ENERGY FROM OTHER MATERIALS, SUCH AS FOOD

GROW

ADAPT TO CHANGES IN THEIR ENVIRONMENT

RESPOND TO EXTERNAL STIMULI

REPRODUCE AND MAKE MORE OF THEMSELVES

SMALLEST LIVING THING
Some ultra-small bacteria measure just 0.009 cubic microns. 150 of these could fit inside an *E. coli* bacteria cell.

Enormous living things
A honey fungus living in the Blue Mountains in Oregon, USA, is thought to be one of the largest organisms on the planet.

VIRUSES

Some people do not consider viruses to be living things because they cannot reproduce on their own. Instead, they need other living things, or hosts, to make more of themselves.

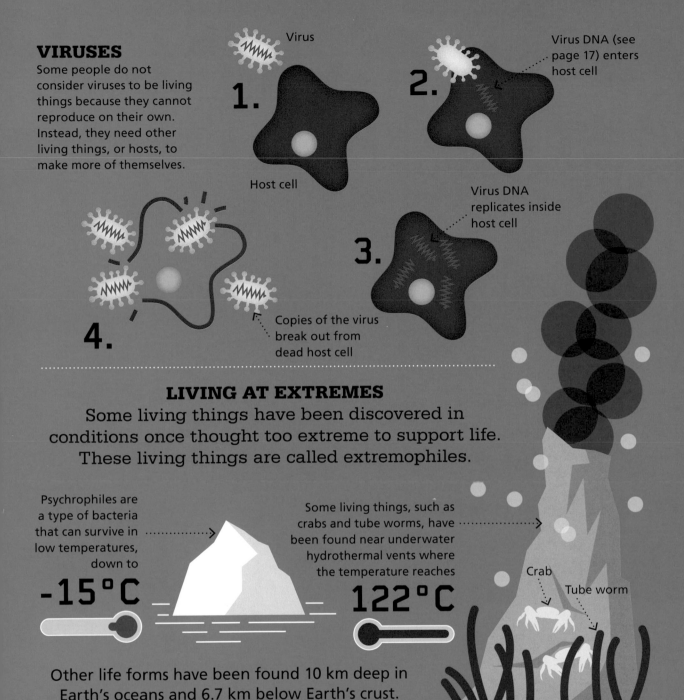

Virus

1.

Host cell

2.

Virus DNA (see page 17) enters host cell

Virus DNA replicates inside host cell

3.

4.

Copies of the virus break out from dead host cell

LIVING AT EXTREMES

Some living things have been discovered in conditions once thought too extreme to support life. These living things are called extremophiles.

Psychrophiles are a type of bacteria that can survive in low temperatures, down to

-15°C

Some living things, such as crabs and tube worms, have been found near underwater hydrothermal vents where the temperature reaches

122°C

Crab

Tube worm

Other life forms have been found 10 km deep in Earth's oceans and 6.7 km below Earth's crust.

It measures 3.8 km and covers **an area of 9.6 sq km** – that's three times the size of Central Park, New York City, USA.

CLASSIFYING LIFE

There are millions of different types of living things on the planet. Scientists have various ways of describing, defining and separating one type of living thing from another.

ANIMALS

PLANTS

FUNGI

TYPES OF LIFE – CLASSIFICATION

Grouping living things together is called classification. Scientists use different layers of classification. Each layer covers a smaller and smaller group of living things, right down to individual types, or species.

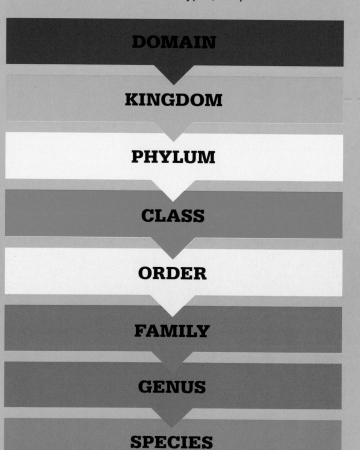

DOMAIN

KINGDOM

PHYLUM

CLASS

ORDER

FAMILY

GENUS

SPECIES

FIVE KINGDOMS

There are five kingdoms of living things. These are:

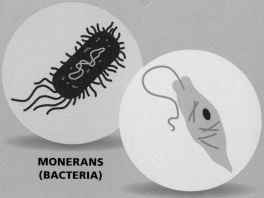

MONERANS (BACTERIA)

PROTISTS (PROTOZOANS AND ALGAE)

Some scientists divide living things into six kingdoms. These are plants, animals, protists, fungi, archaebacteria and eubacteria.

A snail is an invertebrate

A cat is a vertebrate

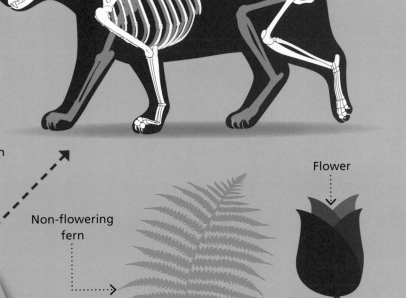

Flower

VERTEBRATES AND INVERTEBRATES

Some animals, called vertebrates, have an inner skeleton and backbones. They include fish, mammals and birds. Other animals, called invertebrates, do not have an internal skeleton and they include insects, spiders and snails.

Smaller and smaller groups

Scientists use several key features to divide living things into smaller groups. These include:

Non-flowering fern

PLANTS WITH OR WITHOUT FLOWERS

Some plants produce flowers as part of their life cycle (see pages 26–27). They include sunflowers, roses and some trees, such as cherry trees. Other plants do not produce flowers, and they include some trees, such as conifers, and ferns.

LIVE BIRTH AND EGGS

Some types of animal, including birds, crocodiles and frogs, lay eggs, which hatch into young. Some of these eggs have hard shells and are laid on dry land, while other eggs do not have a shell and have to be laid in water to stop them from drying out. Other animals, including mammals and some fish, give birth to live young.

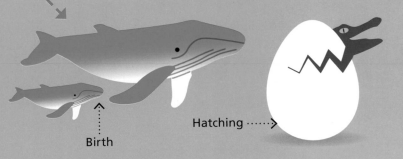

Birth

Hatching ·······>

Some scientists believe that there are 8.74 million different species on Earth. Some studies show that **86 per cent** of land species and **91 per cent** of sea species have yet to be discovered and catalogued.

7

MOVEMENT

Living things are always on the move, whether it's in search of food or water, to find a place to live, to catch something to eat or to escape being eaten.

Walking
Walking involves limbs – extensions of an animal's main body. Some animals walk or run on four legs or two legs, while others have six or even dozens of legs.

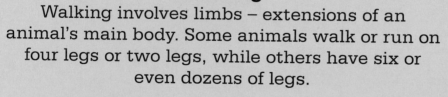

Fold of skin

GLIDING
Some living things have developed the ability to glide through the air over short distances. The seeds of some plants have wings to carry them away from their parent plant, while some lizards, snakes, fish and mammals have folds of skin, which allow them to glide over short distances.

SWIMMING
Because water is more dense than air, moving through the seas, rivers and lakes can take a lot of energy. As a result, many of the animals that live in the oceans have streamlined bodies to allow them to slip through the water as easily as possible.

FLYING

Some animals have developed the ability to fly. Insects have hard wings, which they flap to propel them through the air, while bats have thin pieces of skin stretched between long finger bones to form wings. Birds have wings that are covered with feathers, making them masters of the air.

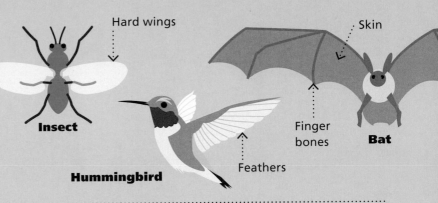

Hard wings

Insect

Skin

Finger bones

Bat

Feathers

Hummingbird

BRACHIATION

Some mammals that live in forests have developed a method of moving through the branches by swinging using their arms. This method of movement is called brachiation.

Slithering and sliding

Land-living animals that don't have legs slither or slide their way over the ground. Snails and slugs move using a single foot that takes up most of their body. They produce a slimy trail to slide over. Snakes ripple their long, muscular bodies along the ground to move forwards.

Slimy trail

Wriggling snake

GROWTH

Throughout their life, living things grow to get bigger and develop from a young immature phase to reach their full size, and also to heal their bodies if they get damaged.

CELL DIVISION

Animals and plants grow by increasing the number of cells in their bodies. The cells divide, creating more versions of themselves, in a process called mitosis.

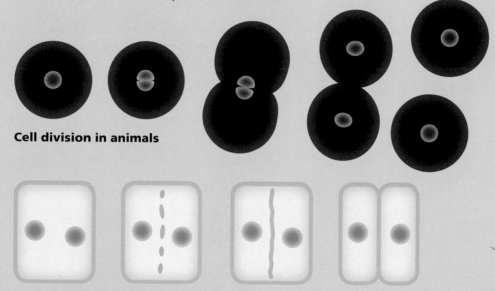

Cell division in animals

Cell division in plants

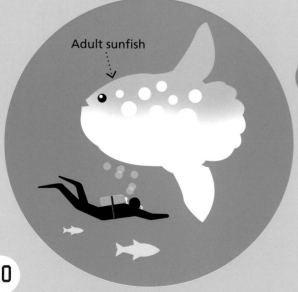

Adult sunfish

Ocean sunfish larva
– actual size

The ocean sunfish grows from tiny larvae weighing a fraction of a gram to about 550 kg, an increase of about

60 MILLION TIMES.

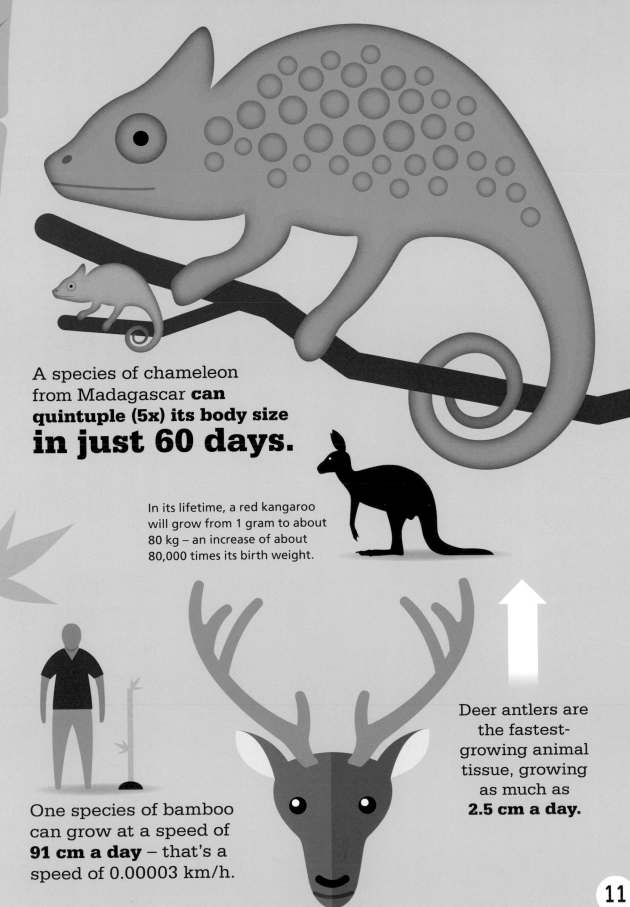

A species of chameleon from Madagascar **can quintuple (5x) its body size in just 60 days.**

In its lifetime, a red kangaroo will grow from 1 gram to about 80 kg – an increase of about 80,000 times its birth weight.

Deer antlers are the fastest-growing animal tissue, growing as much as **2.5 cm a day.**

One species of bamboo can grow at a speed of **91 cm a day** – that's a speed of 0.00003 km/h.

REPRODUCTION

In order for a species to survive, members of that species have to make more of themselves. This is called reproduction, and it can involve an individual duplicating itself or two members of the same species mating to produce offspring.

ASEXUAL REPRODUCTION

Some organisms reproduce by splitting in two or budding, creating smaller copies of themselves. This type of reproduction, which only involves one parent, is called asexual reproduction.

bud

smaller copy

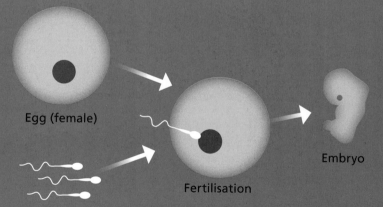

Egg (female)

Sperm (male)

Fertilisation

Embryo

SEXUAL REPRODUCTION

Sexual reproduction usually involves cells from two parents, male and female, joining together to form offspring.

Flowers and some animals have both male and female sex parts. They are called hermaphrodites.

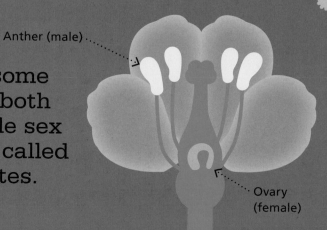

Anther (male)

Ovary (female)

Cloning

Cloning involves making identical copies of an adult living thing. When cloning a sheep, DNA (see page 17) from the cells of an adult is put into an egg from another sheep. That egg then grows into a clone.

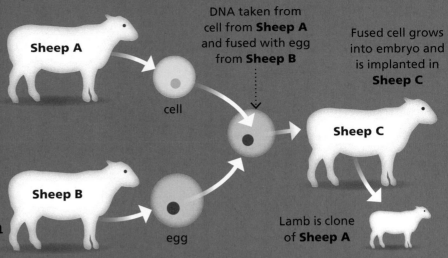

Sheep A

cell

Sheep B

egg

DNA taken from cell from **Sheep A** and fused with egg from **Sheep B**

Fused cell grows into embryo and is implanted in **Sheep C**

Sheep C

Lamb is clone of **Sheep A**

REPRODUCTION CYCLES

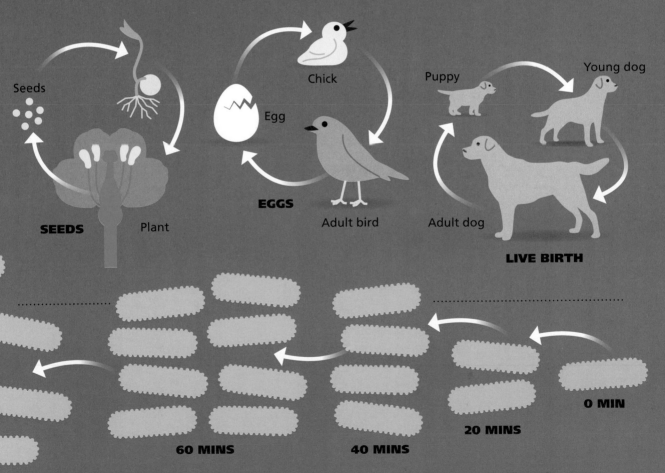

Seeds

SEEDS   Plant

Chick

Egg

EGGS   Adult bird

Puppy   Young dog

Adult dog

LIVE BIRTH

60 MINS   40 MINS   20 MINS   0 MIN

Bacteria are some of the fastest reproducing living things on the planet, with some species doubling their numbers every four to 20 minutes.

BODY SHAPES

Living things come in an enormous range of shapes, from tiny single-celled organisms to enormous trees that tower into the sky. The way these living things look depends on how and where they live.

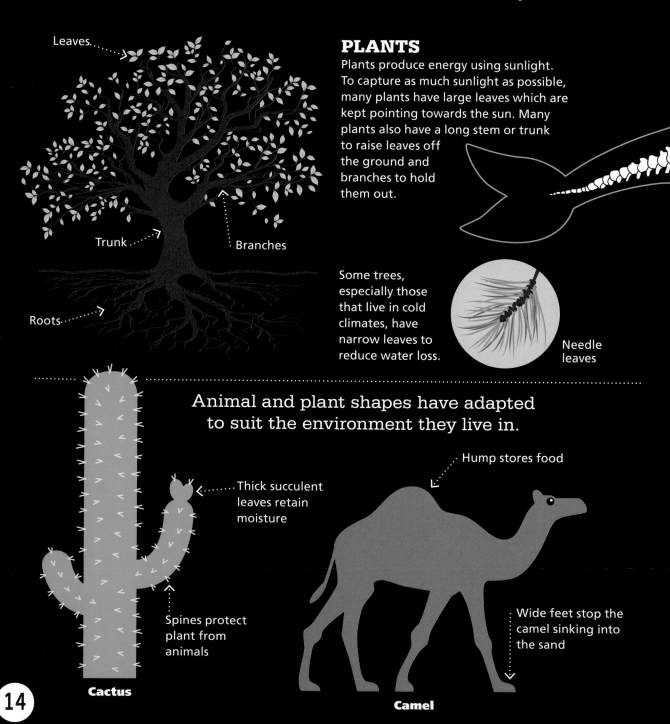

Leaves

Trunk

Branches

Roots

PLANTS

Plants produce energy using sunlight. To capture as much sunlight as possible, many plants have large leaves which are kept pointing towards the sun. Many plants also have a long stem or trunk to raise leaves off the ground and branches to hold them out.

Some trees, especially those that live in cold climates, have narrow leaves to reduce water loss.

Needle leaves

Animal and plant shapes have adapted to suit the environment they live in.

Hump stores food

Thick succulent leaves retain moisture

Spines protect plant from animals

Wide feet stop the camel sinking into the sand

Cactus

Camel

Symmetry

Many living things have symmetrical structures, where one part of the body is related or reflected by another.

Bilateral
This is where one half of the body is reflected by the other half.

Radial
This is where the body is arranged around a central part to produce a circular shape.

Asymmetrical
This is where there is no symmetry to the body at all.

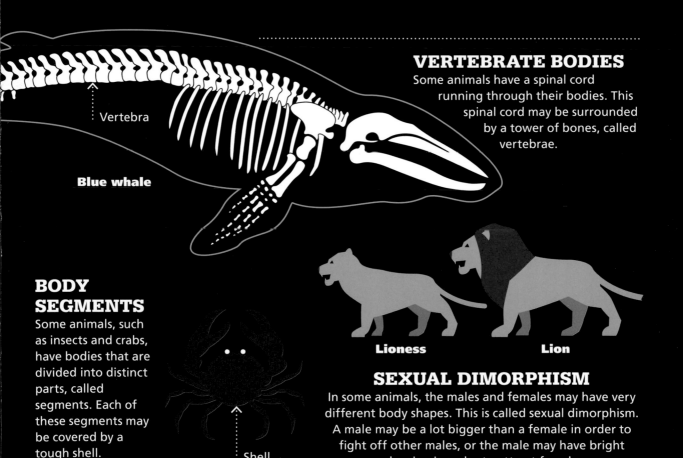

: Vertebra

Blue whale

VERTEBRATE BODIES

Some animals have a spinal cord running through their bodies. This spinal cord may be surrounded by a tower of bones, called vertebrae.

Lioness

Lion

BODY SEGMENTS

Some animals, such as insects and crabs, have bodies that are divided into distinct parts, called segments. Each of these segments may be covered by a tough shell.

: Shell

SEXUAL DIMORPHISM

In some animals, the males and females may have very different body shapes. This is called sexual dimorphism. A male may be a lot bigger than a female in order to fight off other males, or the male may have bright colouring in order to attract females.

Anglerfish

Male and female anglerfish vary greatly in size. The male is tiny compared to the female. When it finds a partner to mate with, the male fuses its body to that of the female.

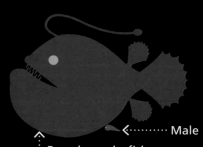

Male

: Female anglerfish

CELLS

All living things are formed of cells.
These are the basic units of life and
they contain even smaller
structures, called organelles,
which allow them to survive
and tell the living thing how
to behave.

Plant cells

Plant cells have a rigid
cell wall. They contain
specialised structures
so that the plant can
produce the energy
it needs to grow
and survive.

Chloroplasts
Found in plant cells,
these are filled with
chlorophyll and use
sunlight to make sugars,
which the plant uses to
produce energy.

Cell wall
Found in plant cells,
this strengthens the
outside of the cell.

Vacuole
This is filled with sap
and it helps plant cells
to keep their shape.

There are approximately
37.2 trillion
cells in a human body.

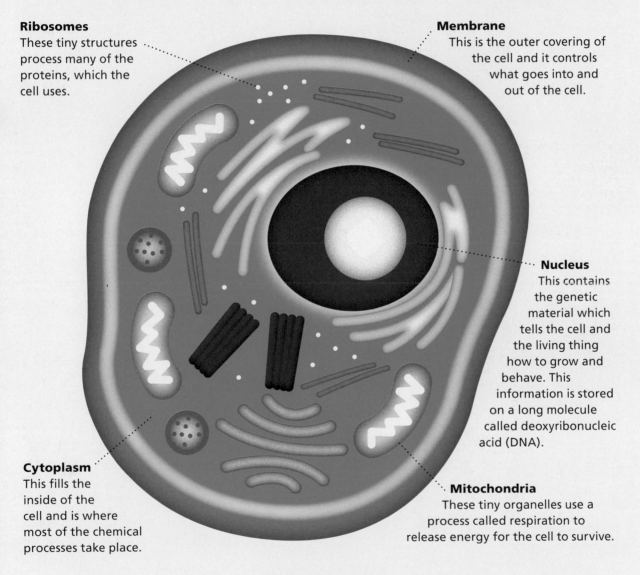

Ribosomes
These tiny structures process many of the proteins, which the cell uses.

Membrane
This is the outer covering of the cell and it controls what goes into and out of the cell.

Nucleus
This contains the genetic material which tells the cell and the living thing how to grow and behave. This information is stored on a long molecule called deoxyribonucleic acid (DNA).

Cytoplasm
This fills the inside of the cell and is where most of the chemical processes take place.

Mitochondria
These tiny organelles use a process called respiration to release energy for the cell to survive.

Animal cells

Animal cells have a flexible covering, or membrane, and can take on many different shapes depending on the role they have to play in the body, such as nerve cells to carry signals or liver cells to process nutrients absorbed by the body.

LIVING TOGETHER

Many living things live in groups. These groups can be small family units, or huge herds containing millions of individuals. Living in a group can offer protection from predators, make finding food easier or can help with the raising of young.

FAMILY LIFE

Some animals, especially mammals, live in family groups where the adults help to look after and raise the young.

Adult meerkats keep an eye out for predators while the young play next to their burrow.

Adult male fights other males that try to take over the pride.

Pride of lions

Lions live together in groups called prides. Each pride has one adult male, with a number of adult females and young.

Female lions do most of the hunting and looking after the young.

Young lions are killed if another adult male takes over the pride.

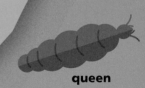

queen

workers   soldiers   king

TERMITES

A termite colony has thousands of individuals. There is usually only one queen and king. Below them are soldiers who defend the colony and workers who look after the termite mound and take care of the young.

18

NAKED MOLE RATS

Naked mole rats live in a colony with about 80 individuals. At the top is a queen who mates with a few males, while the rest are workers.

Queen

Males

Workers

Building a home

Some animals build amazing structures to house their group or colony – some of them even use their own bodies to make a structure!

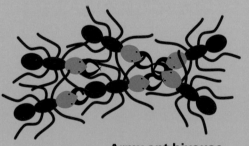

Army ant bivouac

When they are on the move, army ants will link their bodies together to form a temporary shelter, or bivouac, where they can rest before moving on.

Chambers

Tunnels

Termite mound

Termites build huge mounds, some of which can be 10 metres tall. Inside are the chambers and tunnels that form the nest.

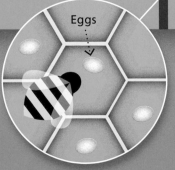

Eggs

Beehive

Inside a beehive, small hexagonal sections form a honeycomb. Eggs are laid inside each section along with a supply of food for the pupa when it hatches.

LIVING IN WATER

Water can be a difficult substance to live in. It is harder to move through than air and deep down in the oceans it produces huge pressures that could crush you instantly.

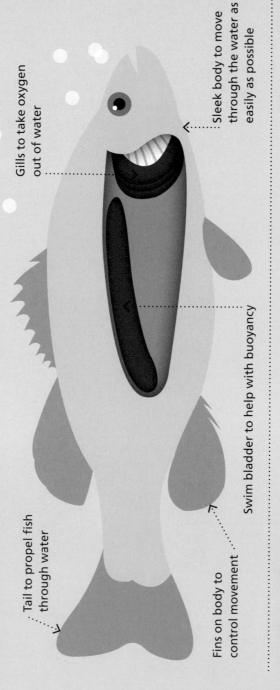

Gills to take oxygen out of water

Sleek body to move through the water as easily as possible

Swim bladder to help with buoyancy

Fins on body to control movement

Tail to propel fish through water

JELLYFISH

Powerful currents keep the oceans moving and many organisms, such as jellyfish, use these to move them about, rather than actively propelling themselves.

SUPER-SIZE

Water can support any organism that lives in it. As a result, some aquatic living things have grown to huge sizes. In fact, the blue whale is the largest animal that has ever lived.

Out of water

Some animals leap out of the water to escape predators or shake off any unwanted creatures, called parasites, or just for fun.

Dolphins leap out of the water to help them move faster using a move called 'porpoising'.

Flying fish jump out of the water and use elongated fins as wings to glide up to 200 metres to escape from predators ...

... that's the length of two football pitches.

Living in the deep

Creatures that live in the dark waters of the deep ocean have developed several body structures to live in the murky depths.

Bioluminescence

Some living things are able to make their own light. This is called bioluminescence and it is used to hide from predators, scare off a hunter or attract prey towards a waiting mouth.

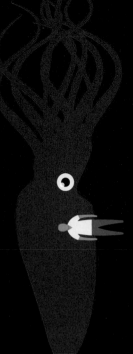

Huge eyes

As it is very dark, some underwater animals have huge eyes to collect as much light as possible.

LIVING ON LAND

Conditions on land can vary greatly, from lush rainforests to arid deserts. Living things have developed many features and behaviours to cope in these ecosystems.

Living with cold
To survive the freezing cold around the poles, animals have developed thick coats of fur and layers of fat.

Living in trees
The trees in rainforests form a dense layer, called the canopy, high above the forest floor. This canopy offers a home to some animals far above predators and a quick way for others to travel through the forest.

Polar bears have a double-layered coat of fur and a layer of fat nearly 12 cm thick to keep them warm.

Finding water
All living things need water to survive, and some go to extraordinary lengths to find this precious liquid in dry conditions. One wild fig tree in Mpumalanga, South Africa, has roots that stretch down more than 120 metres ...

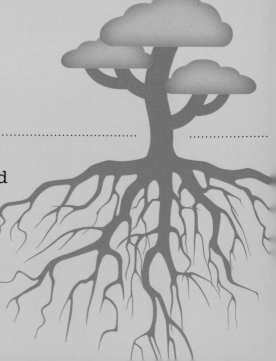

LIVING UNDERGROUND

Beneath the surface, there is very little light and any animals living there have to rely on senses other than vision.

The Mexican blind cavefish has lost any ability to see.

Taking to the air

Being able to fly allows birds, bats and many insects to escape from predators and hunt for food. All of these creatures have wings that can be either hardened body parts, thin parts of skin, or covered in feathers.

Quetzalcoatlus, a prehistoric flying reptile, had a wingspan of

15 metres

making it the largest flying animal to have ever lived.

... which is taller than St Paul's Cathedral, London.

111 metres

Bat wing

Bird wing

Insect wings

FOOD CHAINS AND WEBS

All living things need food in order to survive. While some can make their own food, others need to eat or absorb other living things to get their energy.

FOOD CHAINS AND WEBS

Energy is passed from one living thing to another in a system called a food chain. At the start of every chain is a producer, which is usually a plant. Plants can produce their own energy using sunlight and carbon dioxide. Plants are eaten by animals, called herbivores, which are eaten by other animals, called predators. Several food chains come together to form a food web.

Predators
Meat-eating carnivores kill and eat primary consumers, making them secondary consumers. These secondary consumers may be eaten by other carnivores, who are known as tertiary consumers.

Grazers
Plant-eating herbivores graze on producers, making them the first, or primary consumers.

Producers
Producers use sunlight and carbon dioxide to make sugars in a process called photosynthesis. They then use these sugars along with oxygen to produce the energy they need to live and survive.

Tertiary consumers

Secondary consumers

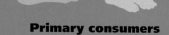

Primary consumers

Sun
Energy

Producers

TROPHIC LEVELS

Each stage in a food chain is called a trophic level. At the start of the chain are the producers and these are eaten by plant-eating consumers, which, in turn, are eaten by meat-eating consumers.

WEBS

A food web has several chains where lots of different species are dependent on each other for the energy they need to live.

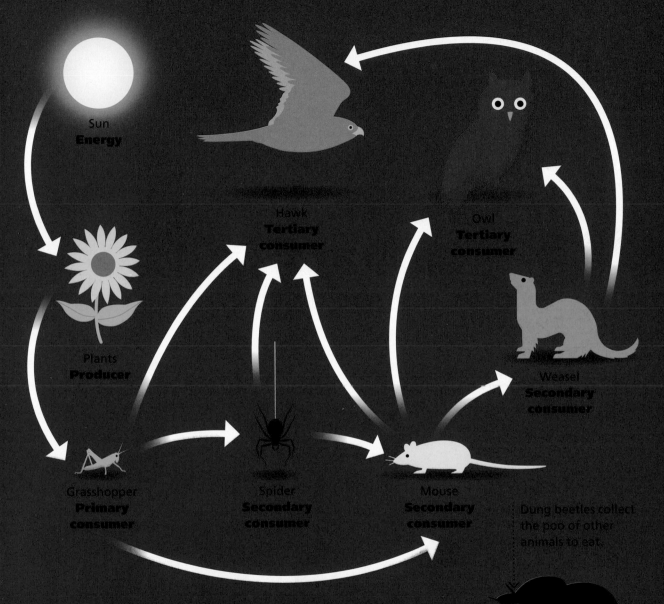

Sun
Energy

Hawk
Tertiary consumer

Owl
Tertiary consumer

Plants
Producer

Weasel
Secondary consumer

Grasshopper
Primary consumer

Spider
Secondary consumer

Mouse
Secondary consumer

Dung beetles collect the poo of other animals to eat.

Recycling

A key part of any food web is the ability to re-use nutrients. This is the job of recyclers and decomposers, who feed on the waste products and dead bodies of plants and animals. They break these down and return their nutrients to the food web, where they are used by producers (plants).

CIRCLE OF LIFE

As many living things get older, they grow bigger, changing from immature offspring to mature adult versions. After reaching maturity, living things grow old and eventually die. This series of changes is called a life cycle.

Plant life cycle

Plant life cycles vary depending on the type of plant.

1. When a seed is ready to grow, it germinates, producing a shoot and roots.

2. As these grow bigger, the plant may produce other structures such as branches, leaves and flowers.

3. Eventually it produces more seeds which will fall away from the parent plant and may germinate to start their own life cycle.

Metamorphosis

Some animals, such as butterflies, go through big changes during their life, completely changing their body shape during a process called metamorphosis.

1. Butterflies lay eggs on leaves so that the young have a ready source of food when they hatch.

4. When the caterpillar has gone through its changes it emerges as an adult butterfly.

3. When the caterpillar has finished growing it forms a pupa, or chrysalis. Inside the pupa, the caterpillar goes through some major changes.

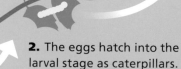

2. The eggs hatch into the larval stage as caterpillars. These start to feed on the leaves.

Life expectancy

How long living things can expect to live varies greatly from species to species.

Common house mouse
4 YEARS

Asian elephant
86 YEARS

Macaw
up to
100 YEARS

Human
longest-living person
Jeanne Calment
122 YEARS

Galápagos tortoise
226 YEARS

**Bivalve mollusc
(ocean quahog)**
more than
500 YEARS

Maturing

As a mammal gets older its body grows, but doesn't go through the major changes of metamorphosis.

Bristlecone Pine
up to
5,000 YEARS

Quaking Aspen
about
80,000 YEARS

A blue whale is about 7 metres long when it is born.

At six months, the whale will have grown to about 16 metres long.

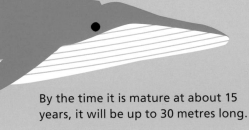

By the time it is mature at about 15 years, it will be up to 30 metres long.

EVOLUTION AND ADAPTATION

Since the first life forms appeared on Earth, millions of species have evolved to live in a huge range of environments in almost every corner on the planet.

NATURAL SELECTION

When many living things have offspring, the genetic material from both parents mixes together to create a brand new living thing of the same species. However, this mixing together can cause changes and variations, called mutations. These mutations could give the individual an advantage over other members of the species, making it more likely to survive and pass on those changes to the next wave of offspring.

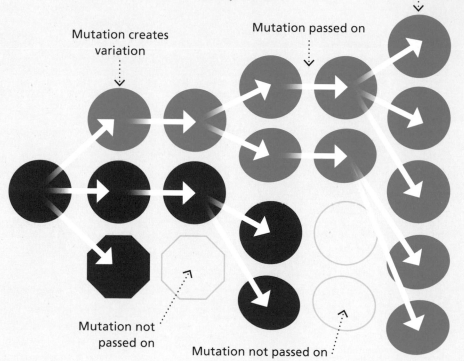

Mutations passed on and reproduced

Mutation passed on

Mutation creates variation

Mutation not passed on

Mutation not passed on

Finches and islands

In 1858, the British scientist Charles Darwin put forward the idea of evolution through natural selection. On a trip to the Galápagos Islands in the Pacific Ocean, he noticed that finches living on the

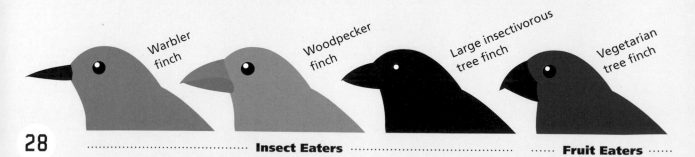

Warbler finch

Woodpecker finch

Large insectivorous tree finch

Vegetarian tree finch

Insect Eaters   **Fruit Eaters**

Extinction

If a living thing is not suited to the environment, then it will die out or become extinct. Extinction can be brought about by:

Dodo

3. Sudden change in climate and conditions

Dinosaur

Darwin's Frog

1. Introduction of new diseases, which the living thing is not immune to

2. Introduction of new predators or competitors

Scientists believe that up to 0.1 per cent of all species are becoming extinct each year. This could be up to **9,000** species every single year.

=100 species

0.1%

More than 99.9 per cent of all the species that have ever lived **are now extinct.**

96%

70%

There have been five major extinction events in the history of our planet. The biggest, the Permian-Triassic event some **252 million years ago,** saw the extinction of **96 per cent of all marine species** and **70 per cent of all land-based vertebrate species.**

islands had a wide variety of beaks. These beaks had evolved to suit the local food source, which varied from island to island.

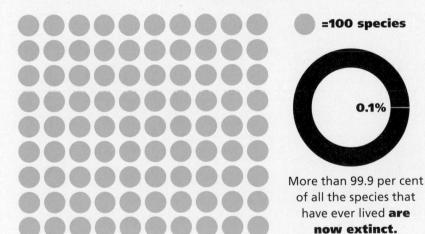

Cactus ground finch

Sharp-beaked ground finch

Large ground finch

......Cactus Eaters......

Seed Eaters

GLOSSARY

adaptation
A feature or characteristic that allows a living thing to live in its habitat.

asexual reproduction
Reproducing and making more of an organism by only using genetic material from one parent.

bacteria
Tiny, single-celled organisms, many of which can cause illness and disease.

bivouac
A temporary shelter.

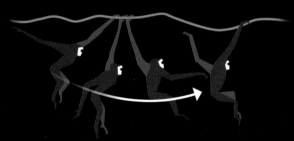

brachiation
Moving through the trees by using the arms to swing from one branch to another.

canopy
The thick layer of branches and leaves formed high above the ground in a forest.

cloning
Creating organisms that are genetically identical to the parent organism.

consumer
In a food chain or food web, a consumer is an animal that eats other living things. Primary consumers eat plants, while secondary and tertiary consumers will eat other animals.

E. coli
A rod-shaped type of bacteria that is usually found in your guts. Most *E. coli* are harmless, but some can cause food poisoning.

ecosystem
The plants, animals and other living things that exist in an area and the relationships between them.

evolution
The gradual changing of physical features and characteristics in living organisms over a long period of time.

extinction
When a living thing dies out completely.

extremophiles
A living thing, usually a tiny microbe, that can live in conditions that were once thought too harsh for life, such as super-hot water.

genetic material
The biological information that describes how a living organism will look and behave. It is stored inside every cell as a long chemical called deoxyribonucleic acid (DNA).

immature
Something that hasn't grown up fully and is still undeveloped.

invertebrate
An animal that doesn't have a spine.

larva
The stage in the life cycle of some living things after they have hatched and before they grow to adult size.

life expectancy

The amount of time a living thing can expect to live for.

metamorphosis

When a living thing changes body shape completely. Many animals go through metamorphosis as part of their life cycle, such as frogs, which develop from tadpoles.

mitosis

A type of cell division where one cell splits to form two cells containing the same genetic material.

mutation

A change in the genetic instructions of an organism which can alter how the organism looks or behaves.

natural selection

A process where living things that are better suited to a habitat will survive and reproduce, while those that are less well adapted will die out and become extinct.

organelles

Small units that are found inside cells and have specific jobs to do.

producer

In a food chain or food web, a producer is usually a plant which uses energy from the Sun to produce energy.

psychrophiles

A type of microbe that can survive in very low temperatures.

sexual dimorphism

When males and females of a species look different from each other.

sexual reproduction

Reproducing and making more of an organism by using genetic material from two parents.

species

A type of living thing whose members have the same characteristics and can breed with each other to produce fertile offspring.

vertebrate

An animal that has a spine.

virus

A tiny object that contains genetic material, but can only reproduce itself inside the cell of a living thing. Many viruses cause disease.

Websites

MORE INFO:
www.bbc.co.uk/bitesize/ks2/science/living_things/
Part of the BBC website which is packed with facts, videos and games about living things.

www.education.com/activity/plants-animals-the-earth/
A website that's full of activities about exciting plants, animals and earth sciences. These practical projects are designed to inspire future scientists.

climatekids.nasa.gov/menu/plants-and-animals/
This website has plenty of facts and activities about living things and the environment.

MORE GRAPHICS:
www.visualinformation.info
A website that contains a whole host of infographic material on subjects as diverse as natural history, science, sport and computer games.

www.coolinfographics.com
A collection of infographics and data visualisations from other online resources, magazines and newspapers

www.dailyinfographic.com
A comprehensive collection of infographics on an enormous range of topics that is updated every single day!

INDEX

adaptation 4, 14, 28–29

bacteria (monerans) 4, 5, 6, 13,

bioluminescence 21
brachiation 9

cell division (mitosis) 10
cells 4, 5, 10, 12, 13, 14, 16–17
classification 6–7
colonies 18, 19
consumers 24, 25

DNA 5, 13, 17

eggs 7, 12, 13, 19, 26
energy 4, 8, 14, 16, 17, 24, 25,
evolution 28–29
extinction 29,
extremophiles 5
eyes 4, 18, 21

feathers 9, 23
fins 20, 21
flowers 7, 12, 26
flying 9, 23

food 4, 8, 14, 18, 19, 23, 24, 25, 26, 29
food chains and webs 24–25
fungi 6

gills 20

giving birth 7, 13,
gliding 8
growing 4, 10–11, 16, 17, 20, 26, 27

invertebrates 7

legs 8, 9

movement 8–9

natural selection 28

organelles 16, 17

porpoising 21
predators 18, 21, 22, 23, 24, 29
producers 24, 25
protists 6
psychrophiles 5

recycling 25
reproduction 5, 12–13, 28, 29
roots 14, 22, 26

seeds 8, 13, 26
species 6, 7, 11, 12, 13, 25, 27, 28, 29
swimming 8, 20

trees 7, 14, 22

vertebrates 7, 15, 29
viruses 5

walking 8
wings 8, 9, 21, 23

ACKNOWLEDGEMENTS

First published in Great Britain
in 2017 by Wayland
Copyright © Wayland, 2017
All rights reserved

Editor: Hayley Shortt
Produced by Tall Tree Ltd
Editor: Jon Richards
Designer: Ed Simkins

ISBN: 978 1 5263 0384 4
10 9 8 7 6 5 4 3 2 1

Wayland
An imprint of Hachette
Children's Group
Part of Hodder and Stoughton
Carmelite House
50 Victoria Embankment
London EC4Y 0DZ

An Hachette UK Company
www.hachette.co.uk
www.hachettechildrens.co.uk

Printed and bound in China

The website addresses (URLs) included in this
book were valid at the time of going to press.
However, it is possible that contents or
addresses may have changed since the
publication of this book. No responsibility
for any such changes can be accepted by
either the author or the Publisher.

MIX
Paper from
responsible sources
FSC® C104740

GET THE PICTURE!

Welcome to the world of **infographics!** Icons, pictograms and graphics create an exciting form of data visualisation, presenting information in a new and appealing way.

9780750278461 — PLANET EARTH
9780750278454 — SPACE
9780750283069 — COUNTRIES
9780750281287 — MACHINES AND VEHICLES
9780750278683 — THE HUMAN BODY
9780750283205 — NATURAL RESOURCES
9780750269049 — THE HUMAN WORLD
9780750283199 — ANIMAL KINGDOM
9780750277792 — SPORT
9780750269032 — THE NATURAL WORLD
9780750279628 — ART AND ENTERTAINMENT
9780750283076 — TECHNOLOGY

9780750298407 — ANCIENT EGYPTIANS
9781526398391 — THE MAYANS
9781526300225 — THE STONE AGE
9781526300249 — THE VIKINGS